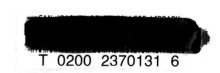

THE NETHERLANDS

SMITHMARK

Text
Nino Gorio

Graphic design
Anna Galliani

Map
Cristina Franco

Contents

Man-made vegetation..*page 28*
North European but fanciful...................................*page 56*
City on the water..*page 78*

1 *Today The Netherlands is one of the most tolerant countries in the world, but in the past ferocious religious conflicts between Catholics and Protestants caused great bloodshed. This statue of Willem V, at the centre of the Binnenhof, the courtyard-citadel of The Hague, overlooked by the governmental offices, dates from those times.*

2-3 *The picturesque lake Kager, north of Leiden, is extremely popular with Dutch sailing enthusiasts. The appearance of this sheet of water has changed greatly over the years, a large part of its surface having been artificially transformed into fertile farming land.*

4-5 *In Spring, with the tulips and hyacinths in flower, the Dutch countryside is an array of bright colours, when the flowers are grown in the open, as on this estate at Egmond aan Zee. In many cases however the floriculture takes place in greenhouses, increasing profits but taking charm from the scenery.*

6-7 *The windmills are one of the most characteristic features of the Dutch countryside: they were invented to provide power for the water pumps that drained the marshy land. Today they are no longer needed and those that remain are protected like historical monuments; some have been dismantled and rebuilt in open-air museums.*

8 *The Stadhuis (town hall) is one of the few buildings in Rotterdam to have escaped the bombing of the last war. The city was subjected to massive air raids, first German and then Anglo-American. Reconstructed the city is today an example of futuristic architecture and can boast the largest port in the world, nineteen miles long.*

9 *The bell tower of Nieuwe Kerk in Delft is one of the landmarks of national identity: in its church are buried the kings of the Orange-Nassau dynasty, rulers of the country since the sixteenth century. Delft is one of the most charming cities in The Netherlands, famous the world over for its traditional blue and white chinaware.*

This edition published in 1997 by SMITHMARK Publishers, a division of U.S. Media Holdings Inc., 16 East 32nd Street, New York, NY 10016.

SMITHMARK books are available for bulk purchase for sales promotion and premium use. For details write or call the manager of special sales, SMITHMARK Publishers, 16 East 32nd Street, New York, NY 10016; (212) 532-6600.

First published by Edizioni White Star. Title of the original edition: Olanda, la terra rubata al mare
© World copyright 1997 by Edizioni White Star. Via Candido Sassone 24, 13100 Vercelli, Italy.

ISBN 0-7651-9313-2

Printed in Singapore by Tien Wah Press.

12-13 *Dutch cheeses, covered with coloured wax, are famous all over Europe: backed by skilful marketing policies, Edam and Gouda - to mention only the most famous - have acquired a solid market share abroad. The dairies, today a thriving industry, have generated folklore, famously expressed at Alkmaar. On Friday mornings the town square fills with men dressed in white: they are local cheese-makers, members of four corporations, who bring their produce on characteristic sleds, used for centuries, and display them on the paving stones to sell to passers-by.*

14-15 *Amsterdam from the air looks like a spider's web. The so-called "canal belt" is formed, from the interior towards the exterior, from Singel, from Herengracht, Keizersgracht and from Prinsengracht.*

16-17 *Middelburg, the capital of Zeeland, claims to have the loveliest town hall in The Netherlands. Unfortunately today's building is the result of a post-war reconstruction; the original, erected in the 1400s in florid Gothic style and adorned with the statues of Dutch counts, was destroyed by a German bombardment in 1940.*

10 top *Texel is the largest and most populated of the Friesian Islands, on which the flourishing farming areas alternate with the natural reserves that protect important areas where marine and marsh birds nest.*

10 centre *An unusual capital, without king or government, Amsterdam is the most fascinating, lively and cosmopolitan city in the Netherlands: its canals, characteristic houses, and special atmosphere make it unique in Europe.*

10 bottom *The picture shows one of the 19 mills that line a canal in Kinderdijk, not far from Rotterdam: all date from the mid-eighteenth century.*

Introduction

The Netherlands immediately conjures up the placid image of windmills, set against the background of a land filled with tulips in spring, with grazing cows in the summer and of frozen canals in winter. A magic country, as is every fairy-tale place: where a little boy called Hans can stop the sea by putting his finger in a hole in a dam. Remember? This story was told in a famous novel, *The Silver Skates* by Mary Mapes Dodge. If you have read it, forget it: because there are many Hollands and not all are fairy-tale.

A list? There is the restless The Netherlands of the painters, who from Rembrandt to Van Gogh have filled 600 museums with their canvases; but there is also the The Netherlands of available sex, that draws masses of tourists to the red light districts. There is the solitary The Netherlands of the Friesian islands, all seagulls and naturalists; and there is the crowded The Netherlands of the *Randstad*, the megalopolis that now embraces a dozen towns. There is the sweet The Netherlands of the flowers, the harsh The Netherlands of the Ajax supporters, the fitness-loving The Netherlands of the millions of bicycles. Lastly, there is a desolate The Netherlands: "a river sediment" as Napoleon defined it, although he had only really seen the odd moor on the border.

But perhaps, to understand the Netherlands we should start farther away. Maybe from Schiermonnikoog, the third last of the Friesian islands for those sailing eastwards. A bleak and windy expanse, it looks as if it has only just emerged from the sea: a few houses, a lighthouse, a pier and thousands of birds, that screech as soon as a wave steps out of line. In other words, all the time: because here, at high tide, nothing is safe, not the houses of men nor the nests of the seagulls. Then comes the ebb tide, and the land takes over again, and miles of sand appear: in fact you can go trekking on the sea bed.

This is The Netherlands: a place where the Bible forgot a verse, that in which God separated the waters from the continents. Here sea and land still have uncertain boundaries; indeed, sometimes they are one and the same thing, maybe at different hours of the day; and even where the dry land is just that, in some cases nine it stretches out below the level of the sea. It is the great Dutch paradox, from which comes all the rest: the Koog aan de Zaan windmills and the canals of Amsterdam; the birds of the Friesian islands and even *The Potato Eaters*, the taciturn peasants of Van Gogh's early works, their faces expressing a thousand foretold tragedies.

Yes, that forgotten verse has had many effects: the first is that The Netherlands has rewritten a Bible all of

its own. It says: in the beginning there was God who created the water; then came man and he created the land. For seven hundred years the Dutch have been snatching acres of land from the sea, using dykes and pumps worked by windmills: the first polders - reclaimed lands - date from the late thirteenth century, the last from the Seventies. But is is not only the sea that gives up acres: those landing in Amsterdam do not realize it, but Schiphol airport is the bottom of a great lake, one that was drained just a hundred years ago.

That the land was created by man is certainly more obvious in Zeeland, a region on the border with Belgium, overlooking a delta that receives the waters of four rivers: the Rhine, Maas, Scheldt and Waal. Down there whole islands are polders, and huge dams control the flow of rivers and tides. Looking at well-kept towns such as Middelburg and Goes, where ash-blonde cyclists pedal between clean houses and fields of forage, all inspires a sense of tranquility; but the people remember the disastrous floods, the last in 1953. Then it took more than the finger of Hans, the little hero of *The Silver Skates*, to stop the sea.

Not even the traditional barriers were enough: that cordon of natural embankments and dunes edging the coast had been devised for normal weather; but one day the North Sea, swollen by squalls and exceptional tides, rose ten feet above its usual level, opened a hundred or so breaches, and inundated the land. This took place on 1st February and it was like the end of the world: the banks collapsed, the rivers gave way, unable to beat the force of the waves; land and water were again one for over a thousand square miles. The outcome: 46,000 homes flooded, nearly 2,000 people dead.

It is just an hour by train from Zeeland to Amsterdam, and everything changes. The colours change: from the green of the polders to a palette of bold hues, decorating the edges of the canals with narrow, oblong-shaped houses, or invading them with rows of houseboats. The people change: the blonde cyclists of Goes become a pot-pourri of different races - their origins ranging from the Moluccas to Surinam. The smells change: the fresh fragrance of Spanish clover is replaced by the sweet-sour aroma of curry, coming from the Indonesian restaurants; or the acrid smell of cannabis, coming from all over, because it is legal here and you can buy it at the grocer's.

Dear, old Amsterdam: few cities have been so loved, dreamt of, or condemned. Leaf through its curriculum: it was the port of sin in the days of the great navigators; port of illusions in those of the hippies; a port of haven for Descartes and John Locke, fleeing from a Europe with too many, suffocating certainties. Amsterdam has always been short on certainties: as could only be for a city born on the water and resting on poles; a city that in its centre has more canals (156) than streets, more bridges (1,292) than traffic lights; a city that starting from its very name ("Dam on the river Amster") declares all its aquatic insecurity.

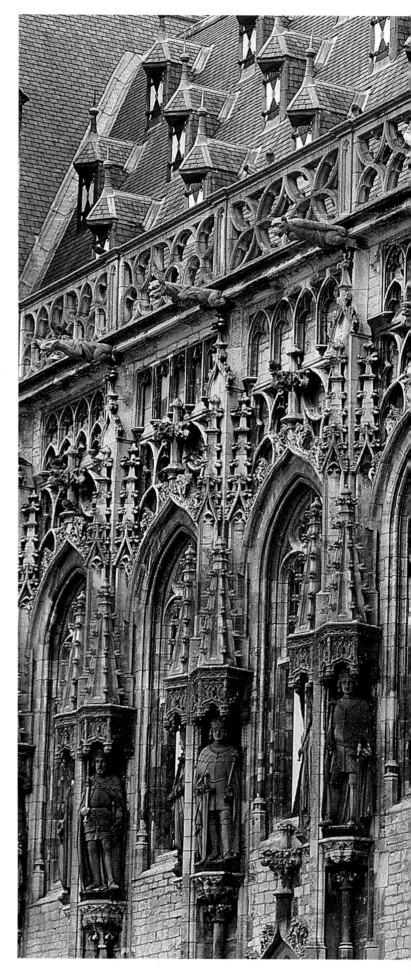

Amsterdam has always acted as a watery, versatile city. Look at the plan of the city-centre: no street is perpendicular to another; it was traced by the canals of the Grachtengordel, which embrace the built-up area in a crescent, the twisted streets fanning out to the Dam, the main square. The capital of The Netherlands is the same in its soul: polyhedric, without harsh corners, capable of embracing all: synagogues and austere Lutheran churches; 7,000 protected monuments and 5,000 prostitutes; museums that are sanctuaries of the European culture, like the Rijksmuseum, and 100,000 immigrants from 150 overseas countries.

It has been called the "Venice of the North" because of the canals; but in many ways it seems more like an Asiatic city: at least in its cuisine, where Chinese rice and *wan-tons* prevail; or at the Tropenmuseum with its splendid collection of exotic art; or in the alleys around the Oude Kerk (Old Church) so reminiscent of Bangkok. Few have resisted the ambiguous, oriental charm of Amsterdam: even Manuel Vazquez Montalban, the famous Catalan thriller writer and inventor of the detective Pepe Carvalho, set his book (*Tatoo*) here, betraying Barcelona for once.

But what has a city like this to do with the The Netherlands of the polders and the neat villages with one foot in the sea? To understand the connection, you must step backwards 400 years: it was then that the Dutchman realized that he made more children than polders and that not even all the acres drained by the windmills were enough. So he started to sail the seas in search of less difficult lands. And Damrak, the narrow harbour of Amsterdam, became the terminal for sailing ships that beat against the frontiers of the known world, tracing new routes.

The "dam on the Amstel" flourished; and the seventeenth century, the "Golden Age", saw the city grow to 200,000 inhabitants: a metropolis for the times. Amsterdam found itself at the centre of the fifth colonial empire of the world, stretching from Indonesia to Guyana; the Jewish quarter of Jodenbuurt competed with Antwerp as the capital of the diamond trade; and a mansion in Oude Hoogstraat was the headquarters of the East India Company, the famous (and notorious) overseas trading company; silk, spices, gold, all was in its hands. The Asiatic Amsterdam, crossroads of exotic fragrances, is the heritage of those times.

Of the empire that was, all that remains today is the odd island in the Antilles, good for rum and casinos. But Dutch names scattered to the four corners of the globe are a reminder of the epic deeds of the sailing ships and their crews. Some examples? The Barents Sea stretches between Russia and the North Pole: it is named after Willem Barents, an arctic explorer from Amsterdam. And in the extreme south of Chile, is Cape Horn, so called by a navigator from Hoorn, Willem Schouten, who was the first to round it. Or again, in Australia, the island of Tasmania is a reminder that the first European seen down there was a Friesian, a certain Abel Tasman.

18 top   In the countryside, especially around Groningen, there are numerous megalithic complexes. Little is known of the Dutch pre-Roman history, which was long: the first human settlements date from approximately 60,000 years ago. The Roman conquest, of 57 B.C., did not affect the whole country, but only the regions south of the Rhine. The effects of that rift are still felt: Dutch is spoken south of the Roman border, Friesian north of it.

18 bottom   Breda, once a powerful stronghold with an important role during the anti-Spanish war, still boasts monuments of considerable interest such as the superb Gothic cathedral and the Stadhuis. Less well known is the Begijnhof, despite being just as picturesque as the far more famous one in Amsterdam: the Beguines, pious unmarried Catholic women, used to live here and are commemorated by this bronze monument.

19 Zwolle, the main town of Overijssel, was once surrounded by mighty walls. Today, all that remains is the impressive Sassenpoort (seen here); its dimensions suggest the power of the city until the 17th century. Today Zwolle is a neat and active provincial town, with the IJsselmer and large Flevoland polders a short distance away.

Even New York, the symbol of English-speaking America, was born Dutch with the name of New Amsterdam. It is a sign of what the epic era of the sailing ships represented; for the world, it meant wider horizons; for the Netherlands, a revolution: the sea, ever a nightmare, became the bridge that led to all - trade, fishing, adventure. The proof of the turning-point? They say that the soul of a country comes through in its fables, because it is in these that every people places its dreams, fears, what counts: the French fables are full of castles, the German ones of woods, the Chinese ones of flowers and nightingales. The Dutch fables speak always of ships.

Let us hear one. It is said that many centuries ago the sea was an expanse of fresh water and the navigators had trouble finding the salt needed to cook and conserve meat. At that time a captain from Rotterdam, sailing on distant oceans, landed on an island unknown to maps and ruled by a sorcerer who had invented a wonderful grinder. At first it did not make much of an impression: it was old, worm-eaten, you would not have given a florin for it. But just give an order and that old relic would start to grind coffee, wheat, anything: even without the raw material.

The captain took a fancy to it: "With that grinder - he thought - I will solve my salt problem". So, without thinking, he stole the grinder from the sorcerer. And as soon as he was off shore he tried it out: "Grind salt!" he ordered. The grinder started to spout white powder: it filled one sack, two, three. Only at the tenth sack, when the ship was giving way under a mountain of salt, did the captain realize that he did not know the formula to stop the magic. All ended in tragedy: the ship sank, taking with it the magic grinder, which is still grinding down there. This is why the sea is salty today.

The legend says no more. But someone, between Friesland and Noord-Holland, must have discovered how to stop the grinder, because in the past fifty years a stretch of sea has become fresh water again. It used to be called Zuider Zee and was a shallow and deep gulf, descending from the North Sea to the gates of Amsterdam: it was swept by impressive tides. These alarmed the farmers, but filled the nets of the fishermen from Volendam and Marken with herrings. Now it has been renamed the IJsselmeer and no longer communicates with the open sea: between them is a gigantic, famous dyke, isolating the former gulf and cutting off its outlet.

The Afsluitdijk is one of the modern symbols in The Netherlands: it took 15 years to build, from 1917 to 1932; and when the astronauts looked down on the Earth from space they saw that it is the only human work visible to the naked eye up there, apart from the Great Wall of China. The dyke starts in Harlingen in Friesland, heads south-west and after 20 miles ends at Den Oever, in Noord-Holland. Two roads run on it, and it is washed by two seas: to the right the Waddenzee, colourless and bad-tempered; to the left the IJsselmeer, bluer and calm, now fresh water because it has become a lake.

Poor IJsselmeer: like all those who are too good it will not live long; the Afsluitdijk was born to isolate and drain it. At first they thought it would take fifty years, then everything went more slowly; but from a tower standing half-way across the dyke you can see that the newly-born lake is already much lower than the sea before it. If the tower were higher and the horizon wider, you would see that the adjacent shoals of the former sea are now wide polders (Flevoland, Wieringermeer) which repeat the Dutch miracle: the banks where soles used to lie now produce potatoes and onions.

But the true miracle of the Afsluitdijk is another: the dyke has halved the distances between the "real" The Netherlands and Friesland, a region that has always been isolated, that has a language of its own and breeds cows of a different race (Friesians). Once, the people of Harlingen had to go all the way around the Zuider Zee to reach the "real" The Netherlands; then - from the sea, as always - came change: just half an hour of dyke and there is Noord-Holland, with its towns: Alkmaar, the cheese capital; Volendam, the fishing capital; Haarlem, the tulip capital. So the Netherlands has become smaller.

Yes, much smaller: because Haarlem is in the Randstad, the heart of The Netherlands, with a string of historic towns: Rotterdam, The Hague, Leiden, Delft, Gouda, Dordrecht and Utrecht. And Amsterdam of course. Of all these, Rotterdam is the most important: it numbers just 700,000 inhabitants but is the largest port in the world, where every year 300 million tons of goods pass. Destroyed in the war, the city was reborn modern, not beautiful; nonetheless, those who look beyond the grey docks find the successor of the Amsterdam of the past, where the The Netherlands of today renews its pact with the sea, no longer for spices but for oil.

The other cities are better conserved and tell the history of the country: a history that is both cultured and peasant, creative and mercantile, a model of tolerance yet marked by ferocious religious wars. So, for a Delft made famous by fine majolica, there is a Gouda that owes all to dairy products. And for a Leiden that lives off the prestige of a centuries-old university there is a Dordrecht that has always survived on river tolls. Or again: Utrecht, a papal outpost, which until 300 years ago burnt witches and heretics, is set against The Hague, ostentatious non-capital, home of the European Court of Human Rights.

What do these seemingly different cities have in common? Many things: the most obvious is a love for art, for painting in particular. The roots of the Flemish school, the only one in Europe able to keep up with Italy, lie in the Randstad: Rembrandt and Vermeer, masters of the "Golden Age" came from Leiden and Delft. The list of Flemish painters is long and touches numerous cities: it started in the fifteenth century, with Lucas Van Leyden and Geerten Sint Jans, born at Leiden and Haarlem. Then Hieronymous Bosch

20 top *Dutch peasants stopped wearing wooden clogs and the characteristic white upturned bonnets a long time ago. Now the traditional costumes are worn only during folklore festivals (as in the picture) and often only to please the tourists. Even decades ago, anyone going to The Netherlands in search of the famous women in bonnets would have found them only in a certain area: the villages of Volendam and Marken, on the coast of Noord The Netherlands, overlooking the IJsselmeer. Strangely, the costume of a small area has, in the collective fantasy, become that of an entire country.*

20 bottom *Even far from the best known areas, The Netherlands has lovely, ancient towns of a clearly medieval plan. An example is Elburg, on the south coast of the IJsselmeer, accessible only by secondary roads.*

21 top *Groningen, the main city in the region of the same name and the most important city in the north, is not on the sea. Just half an hour's drive from the centre and you are in Eemshaven, a village on the coast with a good port: the market of the main city is thus always well supplied with fresh sole and herring. It is not just the fish that makes this town attractive, little-known because off the normal tourist trails: there are some important monuments and, above all, its history is clearly different from that of the rest of the country. Groningen has always had closer relationships with some German towns than with Amsterdam and The Hague: with Bremen and Lubeck it participated in the Crusades with a common fleet and was then a part of the Hanseatic League. Sometimes the old independence can still be felt.*

and (in the sixteenth century) Pieter Bruegel rose from Brabant to Rotterdam and Amsterdam.

Why did it happen right here? Partly because of the Dutch character: they are the most imaginative of the North-Europeans. Partly thanks to the fervour that passed through the Netherlands of the sixteenth and seventeenth centuries: the same incentive that drove the ships towards distant seas also created a desire for culture and status symbols, hence benefactors capable of financing painters and architects. But if the Netherlands has produced Rembrandt and Vermeer, a little of the credit must go to a verse in the Bible, the third verse of Genesis: "Let there be light" said God and there was light. They say that the Creator said it twice over the Randstad.

Or perhaps three times. Only this would explain the fierce light that spreads in the skies of The Netherlands: sometimes dramatic, sometimes captivating, but always to the fore. To understand the importance of this light in Flemish painting look at a veduta by Vermeer: the clear air, the translucent colours are taken from the landscape of Delft. And Rembrandt's *Night Watch*: a canvas like so many others, were it not for that ray falling across it, violently cutting a section of the scene. It seems an impossible light; but on the coast, when the clouds break after a shower, you will observe the same effect.

Of course Dutch art has come a long way since Rembrandt: in the nineteenth century there was the school of The Hague with Anton Mauve and Jozef Israéls; then came Van Gogh and lastly the De Stijl movement, cradle of abstract painters such as Piet Mondrian and Theo Van Doesburg, or of architects of the calibre of Gerris Thomas Rietveld. Yet, despite all this, in the *Wheatfield with Crows*, a desperate masterpiece of Van Gogh's later work, that strange, unreal light returns, descending from a sky half-blue, half-black; a strong, slightly grim light that changes the perspectives and troubles the conscience.

The Dutch conscience appears resolute in its certainties; but sometimes it has violent starts, capable of requestioning everything: including the battle with nature that is the foundation of the country. This happens, on the IJsselmeer, where the fishing is going to ruin because the Super dyke, the national pride, is stopping the herrings. So people have started to doubt: is it right to bend nature to the degree of cancelling a sea? Once upon a time this problem was not raised: it was a case of either coercing nature or being coerced. But now that the war is won, The Netherlands seems almost to want to make amends to the beaten enemy.

And so it happens that at Harderwijk someone has founded a centre for wounded dolphins - right opposite the polders of Flevoland, once a sea, now planted with onions. And on the coast of Leiden - close to Zandvoort, where the unnatural asphalt of a famous motor-racing track cuts through the dunes - other dunes are fenced off, to guarantee tranquillity for the birds and sea daffodils. Parks and protected oases

21 bottom Leiden, the symbol of Protestant The Netherlands (it was the object of a merciless siege during the war of independence against the Spanish), is a lovely, old city, home of the first university of the Netherlands. It is crossed by two arms of the river Rijn and has a port for small boats. The countryside is filled with huge fields of tulips and hyacinths.

22-23 The North Sea, although windy and anything but mild in temperature, exercises an incredible attraction on the Dutch. In Summer its beaches fill with bathers, at least where there are amenities. This is so for Egmond aan Zee, in Noord-The Netherlands, not far from Alkmaar, the "cheese capital". To shelter from the breeze, people take a wind-shield with them but some also take a sunshade.

24-25 Marken is a fishing village on the IJsselmeer, famous for its multicoloured houses. It is a truly strange village standing on an island, yet it can be reached by car. The key to the paradox lies in a recently-built road advancing from the mainland to the sea on an embankment a mile and a half long. That road has also bridged a wider gap; the inhabitants of Marken and their neighbours on the coast were ancient rivals, officially for religious reasons, (Marken is Protestant, the coast Catholic) but actually because of rivalry in fishing.

26-27 Splendid castles can be found in the Dutch countryside. They have mighty towers and dreamlike gardens and ponds; one is the Kasteel De Haar, close to Utrecht. Built in 1762 as a status-symbol for the Van Nyevelt family, it has never been used militarily.

are to be found all over the place: the island of Texel holds the record, with 19 nature reserves; one, at De Koog, was born to protect a nest, just one, of spoonbill *(Platalea leucorodia)*, a wading bird extremely rare in Europe.

No one appreciates nature more than he who has had to fight it. So - strangely - one of the few European oil-producing countries, with "easy" petrol available in off-shore wells in the North Sea, is also the country that makes most use of "ecological" vehicles, alternatives to the automobile. Such are the trains of the Randstad, renowned for their efficiency. Such are the boats packed into the canals. Such are, most of all, the 11 million bicycles in circulation on urban lanes and *fietspad*, the long-distance cycle routes connecting one town to another and providing the country with a network nearly 4000 miles long.

But the most unusual note comes again from the IJsselmeer: a piece of lake, which was to disappear to make room for a polder, will remain. They call it Markermeer, and it is the south portion of the former Zuider Zee: the home of swans, grebes and ducks; its waters feed a protected marsh, the Oostvaardersplassen, a refuge for wading birds. If reclaimed as planned all this would disappear: so they thought again and the new polder project has been abandoned. The Netherlands of today is a little different from the captain who stole the grinder from the sorcerer: it knows how to stop the marvels it has set in motion, once it realizes that they are harmful.

We have come almost to the end of our ride through the Netherlands, after setting out from the waves of Schiermonnikoog, where land and sea are the same thing and nature wages war on the houses of men. There is a special place where we would like to end our journey: just north of Arnhem, it is called De Hoge Veluwe. It is not a village but a national park, all woods, marshes and sandy moorland. Living free there are deer, roebucks and wild boar; but this is not what makes it such a very unusual place. There, the two anomalous passages from the Dutch bible have found a way to live together.

In The Netherlands God had forgotten to divide the land from the water, giving rise to a wild, hostile environment. But he had created light twice, casting the seed for an extraordinary painting. At De Hoge Veluwe, right in the heart of the park, there is a museum of contemporary art, one of the most important in the world; it is called Kröller-Muller, after the noblewoman who conceived it; it houses works by Rietveld, Mondrian, Van Gogh and other - not only Dutch - masters. The point is that their work is paraded in the open amidst wood and marsh; and they strive to blend with the natural surroundings.

De Hoge Veluwe is not just a museum, not just a park: it is the workshop where Holland is experiencing its latest cultural revolution. Perhaps the restless vitality of nature and the creative genius of man can truly live together in peace after all.

Man-made vegetation

28 top *The flat, green fields near Elburg, in Gelderland, are by no means exclusive to this area: nearly 2,500 acres, approximately one third of Dutch territory, appears thus. It is an example of man's intervention to alter the landscape, in this case to sustain cattle farming, one of the backbones of the national economy with huge fields for grazing.*

28 bottom *Giethoorn, a small village in Overijssel situated in a lake area, shows how nature has sometimes conditioned and influenced man's life. The village houses are constructed with local materials: the roofs are made of thatch, rushes and ditch reeds. The traffic between one house and another travels on the water, with rowing and motor boats.*

29 *Afsluitdijk, the long dyke that separates the IJsselmeer from the North Sea, is the largest work performed by man to alter the Dutch landscape: in the future, the IJsselmeer was destined to be entirely dried out to make room for new farming lands, polders. Conceived in 1892 by Carl Lely, Afsluitdijk was made between 1919 and 1932. Eighteen miles long, it is 90 yards wide and rises 25 feet above the waves of the North Sea.*

Land and sea, all one

30 top *The barren and remote Friesian Islands are the extreme outpost of The Netherlands on the North Sea; they symbolize a primeval world where there is no precise boundary between land and water. The archipelago stretches 15 miles from the coast, forming a cordon beteeen the Noordzee proper (left) and the coastal sea, or Waddenzee (right). Although wild and extreme, the Friesian islands are inhabited: Vlieland (to the fore) has 1,000 residents; Terschelling (in the background) has 4,500.*

30 bottom *Texel is the only one of the Friesian Islands to be cultivated: on a totally flat landscape, fertile forage fields alternate with natural reserves where marine and marsh birds nest. Man and nature coexist here peacefully: Texel is one of the leading ornithological sites in Europe despite having large villages such as Oudeschild on its coast.*

30-31 *The work to snatch land from the sea continues: once the IJsselmeer had been isolated from the North Sea with the gigantic Afsluitdijk dyke, the former internal sea (now a lake) has been split up and will be dried in sections. Today a twenty-mile long embankment goes all the way across it from Lelystad to Enkhuizen. According to plans, opposed by the environmentalists, the "sea" to the left of the dyke (Markenmeer) ought to become a polder.*

32-33 *It is not easy to make a polder. It is not sufficient to enclose a stretch of sea within dykes, nor to put water pumps in action, because the machines can only do the bulk of the work, leaving stretches of treacherous salty mud. The rest is entrusted to the painstaking work of man, not so very different from the centuries gone by: wooden trellises are still laid out at the water's edge to harden the mud.*

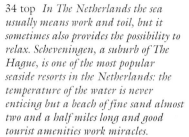

34 top *In The Netherlands the sea usually means work and toil, but it sometimes also provides the possibility to relax. Scheveningen, a suburb of The Hague, is one of the most popular seaside resorts in the Netherlands: the temperature of the water is never enticing but a beach of fine sand almost two and a half miles long and good tourist amenities work miracles.*

34 bottom *The wind on the western coast has with time accumulated sand dunes, lending a characteristic note to the landscape and providing the ideal habitat for wild plants and birds. One stretch of this coast, between Leiden and Haarlem, is now a national park.*

34-35 *After Scheveningen, the island of Texel, on the Friesian archipelago, has also successfully devoted itself to seaside tourism. The best-equipped resort is the village of De Koog, on the west coast, where rows of white cabins stand like sentries on the beach.*

36-37 *Another view of Scheveningen, near The Hague: just like any seaside resort on the Mediterranean, hotels and holiday homes stand just behind the beach.*

When man
is discreet

38 top *Windmills are a typical example of architecture interacting with the surroundings: the large blades used the wind power to work efficient pumps that drained the water from the land, creating arable land and a totally new landscape.*

38 centre *In the northern hinterland of Amsterdam, Zaanse Schans provides an opportunity to see traditional regional architecture: rural houses and five old mills were dismantled and transferred to this large open-air museum.*

38 bottom *Giethoorn, a small village in the Overijssel region, is a model of harmony between scenery and the presence of man. Even the materials used for the houses blend with the environment: the roofs are made in thatch, rushes and ditch reeds. This was not decided by an architect of course - the local fishermen merely used what was to hand.*

38-39 *Scattered over an area of lakes and canals, the houses of Giethoorn are linked by bridges; but because of the very nature of the place, traffic travels almost entirely on the water.*

40-41 *Volendam, just a few miles from Amsterdam, is a picturesque fishing village with traditional brick and timber houses. Today it is invaded by hordes of tourists but its fame dates from the last century, when numerous romantic painters would come to paint the fishermen at work; in the end a colony of artists grew up here.*

42-43 *In the polder area the new settlements sometimes take on bizarre and debatable structures and forms; this is not so of Elburg, a medieval village overlooking the IJsselmeer: its houses are an anthology of traditional styles.*

Land of water

44 top *Stock breeding plays an important role in the economy and indirectly on the order of the Dutch scenery. Large areas have to be used for grazing to feed the 14 million pigs, 5 million cattle and 2 million sheep. This has led to massive forest clearing operations that have created a characteristic uniform, green Dutch countryside with 2,500 acres of meadow land.*

44 centre *The deer in the De Hoge Veluwe national park seem a surprisingly wild presence on the well-controlled Dutch landscape, but this is a partial illusion. These animals were imported centuries ago to adorn the parks of the noble villas.*

44 bottom *It would be absurd to seek glimpses of virgin nature in a country such as The Netherlands, where man has always been short of space. But a curious phenomenon can be seen at Weerribben, east of the IJsselmeer: an area of peatbogs, farmed and then abandoned because not economical, has now been taken over by spontaneous vegetation and has become a national park.*

44-45 *With time, the Dutch landscape has taken on an increasingly uniform appearance: a flat, green plain as far as the eye can see, as near as Elburg, in Overijssel.*

46-47 *Sometimes man's occupations make even more radical changes in the landscape. In the South-West, for instance, the intensive cultivation of flowers has led to the construction of huge greenhouses; seen from the air, these resemble a huge and unsettling "glass city".*

Flat but not monotonous

48 top *One of the most common clichés is that the Dutch landscape, being so flat, is highly monotonous.*
The Netherlands is instead quite varied if seen with an unbiased eye. All it takes is a castle, such as that of Loevenstein, to enliven the panorama and make it attractive. This manor stands in a strategic position at the point where the Meuse meets the Rhine.

48 bottom *Although it has been extensively shaped by the human hand, the Dutch countryside, especially if seen from above, has a fascination all its own. Rows of trees edge the fields forming a chessboard on which the various shades of green alternate in ever-changing effects.*

48-49 *The Friesian Islands are an archipelago in the North Sea and form a cordon off the Northern coast of The Netherlands. This is a world of extremes swept by the wind and tides. In front of the island of Schiermonnikoog (seen here) the ebb-tide is so strong that the water draws back for miles and people trek between the island and the mainland. This is another good reason for not considering The Netherlands boring.*

Water games
on the rivers

50 *The most tranquil of the rivers that
flow into the Delta is called Lek. More
than a river in the strictest sense, it is an
arm of the Rhine, deviating from the
main watercourse on the border between
Germany and the Netherlands.
The Dutch, however, consider it a river
in its own right and have given it a
name of its own.*

50-51 *The mouth of the Zuid-Beveland
canal, near Middelburg in Zeeland,
is one of the main gateways to the
Netherlands via the sea. Via a system
of locks, it leads to the Delta the intricate
weave of waters in which three great
rivers come together (Rhine, Meuse and
Scheldt). This region, once subject to
disastrous floods, has been restrained
in a complicated system of dykes and
locks. This guarantees the safety of the
inhabitants but prevents the passage
of boats on the natural waterways.*

52-53 *Sometimes Dutch "water games" can also serve to wage war. This is demonstrated by Willemstadt, a town in Zeeland with an unusual star plan. It was formerly the fortress of William I, the Sillent, who led the Netherlands' war of independence against the Spanish. In 1583 the architect Adrian Antonisz had the waters of The Netherlands Diep, the large estuary in front of it, re-routed and used them to create an insuperable moat around the town.*

53 *A different town, a different region, but the water games for war purposes remain the same. The picture shows Naarden, in an area close to Amsterdam called Gool. Here, in the 1600s, it was the Spaniards who deviated the waters to create a fortress and keep the rebelling Dutch at bay. Seen from the air, it looks just like Willemstadt even though the flag flying on the battlements was that of the enemy.*

54-55 *The town of Zutphen, an ancient Hanseatic settlement on the banks of the Ijssel, was founded in the 12th century and is dominated by the large cathedral; this houses the "Librije", a library - unique in Europe - dating from the Middle Ages.*

North European but fanciful

56 top *For the Dutch people, the green spaces dotting the urban fabric of their towns play a vital role: whenever the weather permits, much of the day is spent in the open air.*

56 bottom *Living on the water may seem bizarre, but for the Dutch - used to living on land that is not always dry land - it is very natural. Many people in the towns solve the problem of high rents by living on boats. Amsterdam has almost 2,500 house-boats.*

57 *Blonde hair, light complexion, slender figure: this is how we imagine the typical Dutch person, but it is not always so. The colonial past, followed by open borders, have brought massive waves of migrants and these have changed the average features of the population. So, today, girls such as these may mingle in the streets with dark-skinned faces or almond eyes. The largest number of immigrants is found in Rotterdam, where the foreign residents (excluding those who have already obtained Dutch citizenship) total almost 15% of the whole. Data on religious faiths help to convey the meaning of this metamorphosis: Protestants, in the past the core of the independent Netherlands, now account for just 25% of the whole, overtaken by Catholics (34%); but the most curious fact is that 3.2% of the population declares itself Muslim.*

Where polders flourish

58-59 Everyone talks about tulips but the Netherlands are also the leading producers in the world of hyacinths, crysanthemums, roses and fleurs-de-lys grown under glass. Dutch floriculture has a long-standing tradition: in the beginning, about 400 years ago, it was practised not for profit but for prestige; the nobles used to surround their homes with botanic gardens filled with exotic flowers, exhibited as a status symbol. But the botanic gardens became gardens and then fields. The Netherlands has approximately 400 historic "gardens": the oldest is the Clusiustuin in Leiden dating from 1594. Other "cradles" of floriculture are the Haren garden in Groningen and the Plantage in Amsterdam.

59 top The largest public flower market is the Bloemenmarkt in Amsterdam, held every weekday (Saturday included) along the Singel, one of the concentric canals in the old city centre. Partly on street-stalls and partly on boats, in Spring and Summer, the Bloemenmarkt is a riot of colour: cut flowers and plants are displayed over nearly half a mile, giving the district around the Rijksmuseum an inimitable variety of colour. In winter the colours disappear but activity does not stop: it is time to sell seeds and bulbs.

59 bottom As well as the Bloemenmarkt in Amsterdam (seen here), other famous public markets are held at Haarlem, Delft and Utrecht. The most important places for wholesale transactions are, however, Aalsmeer and Honselersdijk. Aalsmeer, south-west of Amsterdam, is the home of the Bloemenveing, the largest flower auction in the world, dealing every day with approximately 14 million tulips, hyacinths and crysanthemums. Similar but with a slightly smaller turnover is the Honselersdijk auction, close to The Hague.

60 Keukenhof is an unusual name for an estate totally given over to flower growing: literally it means "kitchen garden". As always there is a reason: in the 15th century some of these fields belonged to a countess, Jacoba Van Beieren, an enthusiast of vegetarian cuisine who used them to supply her kitchen with herbs and rare spices. Today Keukenhof is one of the largest Dutch floriculture estates: specializing in tulips and hyacinths, it covers an area of 70 acres; six million bulbs are planted here every year and it receives 800,000 visitors in Spring. It is roughly half way between Amsterdam and The Hague, not far from Aalsmeer, the site of the largest flower auction in the world. The most incredible thing is that this floriculture giant did not exist a few decades ago: Keukenhof was founded only in 1949.

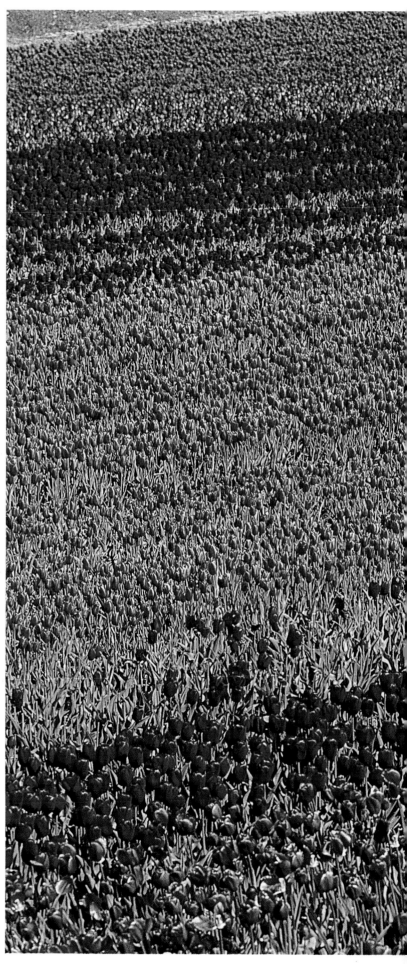

60-61 The best time to visit Keukenhof, as for all the Dutch flower-growing estates, is between early March and late May. In these three months the countryside becomes an endless carpet of flowers, divided into monochromatic sectors. The first to flower are the tulips, the hyacinths reaching their peak from mid-April onwards. The region of Aalsmeer, where Keukenhof lies, is well known for the history of its lands as much as for its flowers. Until a century and a half ago much of the countryside now used for floriculture was a marshy lake, the Haarleemmermeer, which stretched almost to Amsterdam, where today Schiphol international airport lies. Then in 1851 the lake was entirely dried out with the aid of mechanical water pumps and turned into large polders.

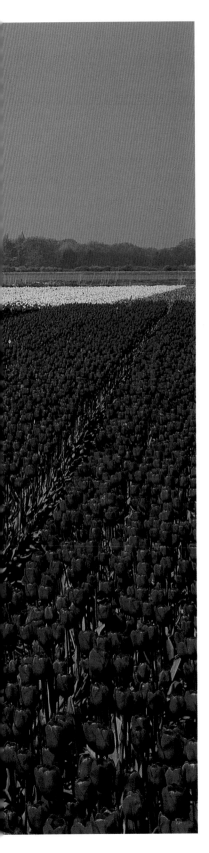

62-63 *Although it is not the only product of the Dutch greenhouses, the tulip is still the symbol of the Netherlands. Over the centuries The Netherlands has selected the best varieties of the species and it is in The Netherlands that its cultivation has reached the industrial dimensions known today. Yet, although the Dutch do not like to be reminded of this, the tulip was not their invention. It is almost certain that Bohemia had it first. A curious dispute exists on the origin of the tulip. Everyone agrees that this flower has ancient oriental origins and that it came to Europe in the 17th century via Turkey. But from this point on there are two versions of the story. The first given credit among others by the Museum voor de bloem bollentreek (Flower Bulb Museum) in Lisse, close to Aalsmeer, says that the first "European" bulbs were imported directly from Turkey by Dutch traders. The second, accepted on the rest of the continent, says that the first tulips in Europe flowered in a garden in the castle of Prague: they were a gift from the Sultan to the king of Bohemia. But those strange and fascinating flowers were desired by all, so one day someone stole bulbs from the flower beds and shortly afterwards The Netherlands started its flower nursery adventure. This may be legend, but it is known that in the 1600s a bulb was worth more than gold, as is demonstrated by a house in Hoorn, on the IJsselmeer, which has an unusual pediment decorated with the image of a tulip. That fresco is a reminder that in 1636 the whole building was exchanged for just one bulb of this exotic flower.*

63 top *Tulips are not only grown in open picturesque fields, that make for such lovely views; large greenhouses are used for early flowering.*

63 centre *As well as Noord-Holland, comprising Haarlem and Aalsmeer, other flower-growing areas are Zuid-Holland (seen here) and Flevoland.*

63 bottom *Tulip growing used to employ a great many people but today it is almost entirely mechanized. Nonetheless this sector provides many jobs especially on the commerical and research fronts.*

All the colours of cheese

64-65 *One of the leading and most picturesque cheese-producing areas is Alkmaar, a town halfway between Amsterdam and Den Helder. A traditional market is held here every Friday morning from April to September: dressed in traditional costumes, the cheese-makers arrange their produce on coloured sleds and take it to the town square (Waagplein), where a 14th-century weigh-house stands.*

65 top *Once in the square, the cheeses are arranged on the paving for sale. Cheese is so important for the economy and culture of this region that Alkmaar has dedicated a museum to it (Hollands Kaasmuseum).*

65 centre *The cheeses, all round, are usually covered with wax in one of three colours: yellow, red or black. Once neatly arranged, they make an attractive and colourful sight. The charm of this market is added to by a carillon inside the weigh-house which plays an ancient melody every hour.*

65 bottom *The Alkmaar cheese-sellers are always dressed in white and wear a coloured straw hat on their heads: blue, green, yellow or red. The colour is a distinctive mark of the four corporations that represent the local cheeses. Every corporation has a well-defined space on the Waagplein for the display of its produce. This means that on market day the square seems painted in sectors, creating a lovely effect.*

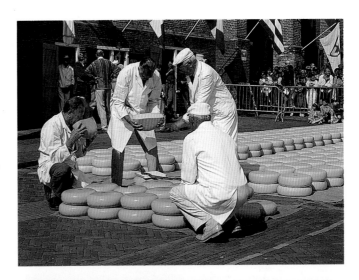

66-67 *Another traditional cheese market, similar to that of Alkmaar, is held on Summer Thursdays in Gouda, a lovely town not far from Utrecht. Again the cheeses are displayed in the square where there is a 17th-century weigh-house. On its facade is a bas-relief depicting the purchase of the dairy produce. Unlike Alkmaar, where only men sell cheese, numerous women can be* *found in the Markt here, wearing traditional costume and head-dress. Cheese making has a longstanding tradition in this area: the first dairies date from the 14th century but the economy really flourished two hundred years later. Today* gouda *is not just a town but also a cheese highly appreciated both in The Netherlands and abroad.*

In the herring villages

68 *Near Volendam, fishing is still conducted with traditional methods, on small motor boats with very long nets, particularly suited to the capture of shoals of herring.*

69 left *Afsluitdijk, the large dyke that separates the IJsselmeer from the North Sea, has not brought luck to the fishermen of Volendam and Marken: the absence of incoming water has impoverished the fish stocks, especially the herring and so the nets are now often left unused.*

69 top right *A fish market is held every morning in Volendam; it sells fresh sole and mackerel. Dutch fish is of excellent quality although less varied than that offered by the waters of the Mediterranean.*

69 bottom *The harbour at Volendam has inspired many painters. The village is picturesque but, in actual fact, exactly the same as a hundred other fishing villages along the coast. It has become more famous than others merely because it is close to Amsterdam.*

The Netherlands is a life-style

70-71 *Dutch children are said to be born on bicycles, ready to start pedalling. Although this may not be exactly true, it is not far wrong: the bicycle is the most popular private means of transport in the Netherlands, at least in the towns. This is confirmed by the figures: on a national scale the 15 million inhabitants circulate on 11 million bicycles; Amsterdam alone has 700,000 inhabitants and 500,000 bicycles. The nature of the terrain, with no hills, favours this use, although this counts only up to a certain point as the wind - sometimes very strong - can be worse than hills. There are other more important factors: every city (Amsterdam and Delft are examples) has a closely-knit system of cycle routes (4,000 miles), trains always have bicycle-wagons, and safe cycle-routes,* fietspaden, *link one town to another.*

71 top *Open-air bands - such as that seen here at Delft - are not exclusive to The Netherlands; nonetheless they are a regular Sunday morning occurrence in the good weather.*

71 centre *The Dutch love to spend their spare time in the open air, not necessarily practising sports. Numerous green areas have become meeting places. For the inhabitants of Amsterdam one of the favourite places for leisure-time is Vondelpark, a garden just outside the old city centre. All sorts of events are held here: concerts, children's games, chess tournaments. People can sometimes be seen spending their Sundays here hunched over a chessboard with a patience that is surprising for such a bubbly city.*

71 bottom *Diamond-cutters need even greater patience than chess players. This is no hobby however: until the last war Amsterdam was the most important place in the world for diamonds. This sector was traditionally controlled by the Jews, but after the Holocaust the sector lost its former importance and Antwerp has become the world leader. Many cutting workshops remain, the best known being that of Gassan Diamonds, active since 1879.*

72 top *The prosperity of The Netherlands is founded on trade with distant countries and, deep down, the Dutch are still traders. This ancient merchant's spirit is expressed, more than in the modern shopping centres, in the flea markets, where small (and sometimes delightful) second-hand pieces end up at the centre of inflamed negotiation. Every town has a weekly market and one is held every day, Saturdays included, in Amsterdam at Waterlooplein; it is always crowded.*

72 bottom *Water is everywhere: dams, locks, floods and tides have conditioned the lives of the Dutch people. The canals and sheets of water all over the country also provide amusement: this is so for the Het Nieuwe Meer, on the outskirts of Amsterdam, a training ground for oarsmen and canoeists.*

73 top *In the Dutch countryside animals are still widely used to draw carts. Despite the high income and excellent road networks, the Dutchman avoids using the car whenever possible. This impression is confirmed by statistics: there are 5,755,000 cars registered in The Netherlands, one for every 2.6 inhabitants. This is the lowest figure in the European Union: France has one for every 2.3 inhabitants while Germany, Great Britain and Italy have one for every 2.*

73 bottom *When it comes to transport, if the passage is from pedals to engine, the Dutch preference is again for two wheels. There are about 500,000 motorcycles registered in The Netherlands.*

74-75 *On Summer Sundays the Vondelpark in Amsterdam fills with spectators for the now traditional open-air concerts. Not always, however, has the park been the scene of carefree musical appointments: at the end of the Sixties it was a reference point for youthful protest, used for enflamed meetings and demonstrations.*
A little like the Latin Quarter in Paris or the Kreutzberg in Berlin it is essentially Dutch, being green.

75 *Tolerance is an essential part of Dutch life and this is particularly evident in Amsterdam, one of the freest cities in the world; it is common to see respectable-looking people mixing in the same streets with those from the "alternative" culture. Here everyone can do his own thing as long as he respects other people's privacy.*

76-77 *It is almost a cliché to think that in Winter the canals could become skating rinks. No doubt it happens but less often than would be imagined. The higher average temperature means that some canals no longer freeze over and others do so only for brief periods. Nonetheless, the sight of the skater gliding past a windmill is one of the loveliest Dutch winter scenes.*

City on the water

78 top *Leiden, Rembrandt's birthplace and home of an ancient university, is to a certain degree the "moral capital" of Protestant The Netherlands. Between 1573 and 1574, during the long religious conflict known as the "Eighty Years' War" it was besieged by the Spanish Catholic troops but resisted beyond all conceivable expectations. In the end, starving and exhausted, it was freed by the Protestant army. Still today, in October, the end of the "year of hunger" is celebrated with ceremonies and banquets.*

78 bottom *Haarlem, the principal city in Noord-Holland, is known as "little Amsterdam" because of its characteristic houses with tall, narrow facades, reminiscent of those of the capital. At the centre of an intense tulip-cultivating area, the city is the home of a flower market that has made it the symbol of The Netherlands.*

79 *The Domtoren in Utrecht is the highest ancient tower in The Netherlands:*
it measures 360 feet and has 465 steps to the top. It was built between 1254 and 1514 as the cathedral tower (Domkerk), the most important for Dutch Catholicism. In 1674, part of the church collapsed in a storm: for this reason the Domtoren now rises solitarily with its florid Gothic lines above the houses of the city. Utrecht is still the home of the only Catholic bishop in the Netherlands.

Amsterdam, reverie on the water

80 top left *Centraal Station is the terminal of the highly efficient Dutch Railways and for many the gateway to Amsterdam. Built in 1889 on three islands, the station- with its neo-Renaissance lines - stands on the Damrak, the main street in the old city centre; this flanks the picturesque quay of the same name and leads to Dam Square. On the other side of Centraal Station, northwards, lies the large modern port called Ijhaven.*

80 bottom left *At the centre of the Nieuwmarkt (new market) stands the Waag, the 15th-century weigh-house.*

80 right *St Nicolaaskerk is the largest Catholic church in the city; it is monumental but little attended. Amsterdam is a Protestant but, above all, a secular city. Near the church stands a tower, Schreierstoren (the weeping tower) where the women used to say goodbye to the sailors about to embark.*

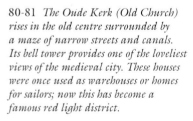

80-81 *The Oude Kerk (Old Church) rises in the old centre surrounded by a maze of narrow streets and canals. Its bell tower provides one of the loveliest views of the medieval city. These houses were once used as warehouses or homes for sailors; now this has become a famous red light district.*

82-83 *The unusual plan of Amsterdam can be best appreciated from the air: the huge Rijksmuseum (at the centre of the picture) marks the boundary between the recently-constructed districts (in the foreground) and the Grachtengordel (in the background), a series of concentric polygons that embrace the medieval centre with surprising regularity. Each polygonal circle corresponds to a canal. The Grachtengordel town was designed thus in the 17th century, Amsterdam's "golden age".*

84-85 *The Kononklijk Palais (Royal Palace) dominates the Dam, the main square in Amsterdam. This building was built in the middle of the 17th century by Jacob Van Campen and was originally the town hall. Only since the last century has it been the official home of the ruling family who live, however, in The Hague.*

85 left *Although it may not seem so, the Royal Palace is erected on piles: it rests on 13,659 poles pushed into a marshy bed. The area was protected by dams to permit the construction of the building; the adjacent square (in the background) is called Dam for this very reason.*

85 top right *The Baroque facade of the Royal Palace is decorated with statues by Artus Quellijn portraying oceans and continents: a reference to Dutch colonial power three hundred years ago.*

85 centre right *Inside the Royal Palace is the magnificent Burgerzaal (Citizens Hall) created to house the town assemblies. This hall rises to the equivalent of four floors of a normal building and is decorated with numerous Baroque statues.*

85 bottom right *The opulence - especially in the interiors - of the Royal Palace, then used as the town hall, led Louis Napoleon, the French King of The Netherlands, to expropriate the building in 1808 and make it one of his homes. At the end of the Napoleonic era, with regained independence, the palace was passed to the Dutch royal family.*

86 top *156 canals cut through the centre of Amsterdam: the narrowest are of medieval origin, the widest, such as this one, are part of the Grachtengordel, the 17th-century network.*

86 centre *2,500 boats are moored in the canals of Amsterdam and are used as house-boats, with their own postal address, electrical connections and sometimes even telephone lines. These are also to be seen in the more elegant districts. This one is anchored on the Keizergracht.*

86 bottom *The "bateaux-mouche" have an entirely different function; these are characteristic wide, low boats based in the Damrak, the dock opposite the railway station, once the city's only port. These vessels are used along the canals for guided tours of the "Venice of the North". The tours are always crowded as the best views of Amsterdam are those seen from the canals. The boats are low so as to pass under the many bridges: the old city centre has almost 1,300 of these.*

86-87 *The homes of Amsterdam are constructed in a characteristic style which has evolved over the centuries without losing certain essential features: the houses are always tall and narrow, with a pointed pediment. A look at the pediment alone will provide indication of the date of the building: if it has a large stepped profile the house was built in the 17th century, if it is necked or bell-shaped (like the three in the picture) it was constructed in the 18th century. Nearly 7,000 of the houses in Amsterdam have been subjected to architectural-cultural restrictions.*

Lights on
the water

88 top *Amsterdam is a lively city even by night, when the bridges in the old centre come alive with a thousand flashing lights. The most crowded area is always the district around the Oude Kerk, which - apparently in peaceful coexistence with church-goers - has the largest and most famous sex supermarket in Europe, now a tourist attraction. The famous "girls in the window" of tolerant The Netherlands are all in these streets. It has been calculated that between 5,000 and 6,000 prostitutes work in Amsterdam - a European record.*

88 bottom *Of all the bridges in the city, the Magere Brug (Skinny bridge) is the most characteristic; this crosses the river Amstel close to the Jewish quarter. Built in 1671, it is the only remaining wooden drawbridge built with the traditional counterweight system, once prevalent. Not far from here is the much visited house of Anne Frank, the Jewish girl who died in a Nazi concentration camp and whose diary has moved readers the world over.*

88-89 *The modern port of Amsterdam (Ijhaven) is in the northern part of the city, running for miles along both banks of the Het Ij, the arm of the internal IJsselmeer. The naval power of Amsterdam reached a peak in the 17th century when all the gains of a great colonial and commercial empire arrived here. Although of impressive dimensions, this port is of relatively little importance, at least if compared with that of Rotterdam, the largest in the world.*

90-91 *The Amsterdam Historical Museum, housed in the ancient orphanage, tells the story of the city from its foundation to the present day; among other things it exhibits numerous canvases depicting the members of the civic guard. This prestigious military corps originated in the 14th century and the first canvas was commissioned in or around 1530. The tradition was carried forward until 1650.*

91 top *The most important museum in Amsterdam and, indeed, all The Netherlands is the Rijksmuseum: this conserves 5,000 paintings and 30,000 sculptures alone. The collections are divided into three sections (paintings, sculpture and history), of which the first is by far the most important; it is an anthology of the leading Flemish painters right up to the great 17th-century masters. Although the international renown of the Rijksmuseum is based essentially on its masterpieces, this "king of museums" should also be observed from without. The neo-Renaissance-style building dates from the end of the last century and its pompous monumentality is remarkable.*

91 centre *Dutch history is not made of painting alone: an important place is held by navigation. This makes the "Rijksmuseum Nederlands Scheepvaart" or maritime museum also very popular; it displays models of period sailing boats, marine paintings, documents and instruments connected with life on board ship. The whole Dutch naval story is told in 30 rooms.*

91 bottom *The collection of paintings portraying the members of Amsterdam's civic guard - more than 50 canvases covering a period of 120 years - are housed in a covered passage linking the history museum to the Begijnhof, a true oasis of peace and tranquility in the heart of the metropolis.*

92 top *The Rijksmuseum is almost entirely given over to Dutch art, from the early Flemish painters to the 17th-century Masters. Among the many works displayed, the most famous is certainly "The Night Watch", in which Rembrandt formally used a laudatory theme dear to the painting tradition of the times and overturned the aesthetic canons in force with the aid of a dramatic and disturbing light.*

92 bottom *Vincent Van Gogh is the greatest and most famous of modern Dutch painters. Amsterdam has dedicated one of its most important picture galleries to him: the "Rijksmuseum Van Gogh". This houses a collection that includes 230 paintings and 550 drawings by the master, some very famous. The "Irises" is one of the many examples of still life painted by Van Gogh in one of his most fruitful periods, which he spent in Paris between 1886 and 1888, before settling at Arles first and then St. Rhémy.*

93 *The famous "Self Portrait with Grey Felt Hat", of 1887, is also conserved at the Rijksmuseum Van Gogh. This is one of the many self portraits by the master: perhaps the best known together with that "with a Straw Hat" painted in the same year and also exhibited in the Amsterdam picture gallery. Vincent Van Gogh, born in Zundert in 1853, lived in Drenthe and The Hague before going to Antwerp and then to France. After a troubled and desperate life, he committed suicide at Auvers-sur-Oise in 1890. It is hard to place his artistic career in a specific art movement: pupil of the Dutch painter Jozef Israéls, in Paris he came into contact with and was influenced by the Impressionists, although he broke away from them to follow his own path. The abundance of self portraits left by him are not a sign of egocentricity but the indication of the painter's poor economic conditions. During his life Van Gogh managed to sell just one canvas and could not afford to pay models, so he painted himself.*

Haarlem, an ancient flavour

94-95 *By no means the oldest nor the loveliest church in the city, the Catholic Cathedral of Haarlem is the most striking when seen from the air. The cathedral is less than 100 years old: it was built between 1898 and the beginning of this century to a design by Joseph Cuypers.*

95 top right *The city's historic cathedral is the 14th-century Protestant Grote Kerke rising in the city-centre. It has a famous organ that was played by Mozart, Listz and Schubert.*

95 centre left *Overlooking the Grote Markt, the main square, is the 17th-century Vleeshal, a former slaughterhouse and now a symbol of the city. The famous tulip market is held in front of this building.*

95 centre right *Haarlem town hall (Stadt Huis) dates from the 14th century but was retouched in 1630.*

95 bottom *Laurens Coster is the pride of the town; this bell ringer lived between 1370 and 1440 and seemingly invented printing before Gutenberg. A monument has been erected to his memory on the Grote Markt.*

96-97 *The interior of the Grote Kerke is remarkably sombre and highlights the Gothic lines of the church. The ceiling is in cedarwood and is supported on 28 massive columns.*

In the land of the flowery castles

98-99 *One of the most romantic castles in the Dutch countryside is that of Haarzuilen; built in the 12th century, it was destroyed in 1672 by the French. Joseph Cuypers restored it to its original form at the end of the last century.*

99 *Another famous castle is that of Muiderslot, near Muiden, south-east of Amsterdam. This was built by Count Floris V in the 12th century to defend the area between the river Vecht and the sea, the "antechamber" of Amsterdam, and was extended over the years. In actual fact, it served more as a meeting place for court intellectuals than for military purposes.*

Utrecht, the other half of The Netherlands

100-101 Just a few dozen miles from each other, Utrecht is very different from Amsterdam, as a glance from the air shows. The bright colours of the capital give way here to dull, slightly gloomy tones and a squared road network replaces the curved lines of the Grachtengordel. Utrecht is far more austere than its older sister of course, but by no means monastic: bustling with initiative, it is today the temple of the Dutch consumer culture, boasting the largest shopping centre (Hoog Catharijne with 180 shops) and trade fair area (Jaarbeurs) in the Netherlands.

101 left Waterways flow between the houses of Utrecht as well: the main one is the Oudegracht, cutting the old centre from north to south and touching the famous Gothic Domkerk cathedral.

101 top right In the heart of the city, the Oudegracht is crossed by nine bridges that link two busy pedestrian zones full of shops. Especially famous here are the goldsmiths' shops on the Minnebroederstraat.

101 bottom right Beside the Domkerk stands the Renaissance facade of the famous University built in the 14th and 15th centuries. The building also has an ancient monumental hall, former home of the canonical chapter-house, where every year the academical year is inaugurated.

Leiden, mythical freedom

102 top left *The most characteristic pinnacle of Leiden is not a bell tower but the tower of an ancient hospital dedicated to St. John.*

102 centre left *The entrance to the city fortress is decorated with the emblems of local noble families, involved in the strenuous defence of the city during the 1573-74 siege, which made Leiden a symbol of independence.*

102 bottom left *The Burcht, the ancient city fortress built in the 12th century, stands on an artificial hill at the point where the two arms of the Rijn, the river that crosses the old centre, meet.*

102 right *As in most of the Dutch towns the characteristic stalls of street-traders are a common sight here.*

102-103 *Despite being far from the sea, Leiden has a harbour for small boats, built on the Rapenburg canal.*

The Hague, governmental seat but not capital

104 top left *Dragons and other monsters adorn the fountain in the Binnenhof courtyard, the complex of government buildings (former citadel of the Counts of The Netherlands) which occupies the centre of The Hague.*

104 centre left *The Binnenhof forms a closed square with access through monumental gateways like the Grenadierspoort (Grenadiers gate) and the Gevangenpoort (Prison gate).*

104 bottom left *There is free access to the Binnenhof on foot or by bicycle, it being a pedestrian area.*

104 right *In the heart of The Hague the equestrian statue of King William II (1792-1842) dominates the Buitenhof, a wide space serving as an antechamber to the Binnenhof.*

104-105 *Situated in the centre of the Binnenhof the Ridderzaal (Hall of Knights) is one of the most bizarre buildings in The Hague: it looks like a church but is actually a 13th-century civil building, formerly used as a throne room. Today it houses the plenary gatherings of the Parliament. Once a year, in September, the Ridderzaal is the scene of a beautiful ceremony, when the Queen arrives in a carriage to inaugurate the new session of Parliament.*

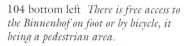

106 top left *The gate in front of the Paleis Noordeinde, the Queen's residence in The Hague, carries the royal coat of arms. The royal family is extremely popular in The Netherlands, mainly for a life-style that avoids pomp and is egalitarian and profoundly democratic. It is not uncommon to encounter Queen Beatrix shopping in the streets of the city like any other busy Dutch woman.*

106 right *The Oude Stadhuis, the ancient city hall, is an elegant mansion built between 1564 and 1565 in a style strongly influenced by the Italian Renaissance. The building was later extended and altered in the 18th century.*

106 bottom left *The unusual city emblem shows a stork, a bird commonly seen in the Netherlands.*

106-107 *The Paleis Noordeinde is an elegant 17th-century building standing in the heart of the city; seen from the outside, it is hard to conceive that this is a royal residence; however in The Netherlands respect for the privacy of the Queen and her family is considered natural. The acknowledged moral leadership of the House of Orange over the country is manifested by truly enviable esteem and fondness on the part of the people.*

108 top *The Hague is the home of one of the major picture galleries in The Netherlands, second only to the Rijksmuseum in Amsterdam. Officially it is called the Koninklijk Kabinet Van Schilderijen Mauritshuis, although it is usually referred to as the Mauritshuis from the name of the 17th century general who lived in the palace now housing the museum. Its most popular room is number 14, where one of Rembrandt's most famous paintings is on show "The Anatomy Lecture of Dr. Nicholas Tulp". Other paintings by Rembrandt kept in this museum are "Susannah at the bath", "Two Moors", "The Presentation at the Temple", "Homer", "Saul and David" and the famous "Self Portrait with Feathered Cap".*

108 bottom *The Mauritshuis has 16 rooms in all; it has paintings by many other famous painters besides Rembrandt, including the 15th-century Flemish painter Rogier Van der Weyden ("The Lamentation of Christ"), Pieter Paul Rubens (various portraits) and Jan Vermeer ("View of Delft" and "Girl in a Blue Turban"). The museum has a thousand or so canvases, only half being on show to the public. The collection was created immediately after the fall of Napoleon, when some of the pictures, plundered by the French from the Flemish nobility, were returned to The Netherlands.*

108-109 *A treasure-chest of precious paintings, the Mauritshuis is also of interest in itself, thanks to its attractive and unusual architecture: the building reveals a Palladian influence totally uncommon in The Netherlands. Adjacent to the governmental buildings of the Binnenhof, it was constructed between 1636 and 1646 by the architect Jacob Van Campen as the private residence of general John Maurice of Nassau.*

Delft, famous chinaware

110-111 *Ancient houses in neat rows, a maze of roads and canals and mighty bell towers; this is how Delft appears from the air. To the left is the Stadhuis tower (town hall), to the right, in the background, the leaning one of the Oude Kerk, where the mortal remains of the great painter Jan Vermeer were laid to rest.*

111 top left *Numerous waterways cut through the town centre, the most important being the Rijn-Schie Kanaal.*

111 right *Blue and white are the characteristic colours of the famous Delft chinaware. "De Porceleyne Fles", one of the first factories on the continent (founded in 1653) is still active.*

111 bottom left *The Markt, the main square in Delft, is one of the largest in The Netherlands; overlooking it are the Stadhuis and the Nieuwe Kerk, a Gothic church of the 14th-16th centuries where the remains of the kings of the Orange-Nassau families are buried.*

112-113 *The present Renaissance-style Stadhuis in Delft dates from 1618; it was built on the ruins of a 14th-century building destroyed in a fire.*

113 top right *The highest tower in the town is that of the Nieuwe Kerk, rising to 390 feet. It took exactly 100 years to build, from 1396 to 1496, but some time later it was destroyed by fire in just one night. Restored in the last century it was completed in 1876. A 17th-century carillon still plays inside it.*

113 centre left and right *The loveliest buildings in the town stand on the Oude Delft road, flanking the Schie canal. Here, among convents and ancient residences, is the splendid Gemeenlandhuis, a 16th-century home that has a facade decorated with the arms of ancient noble families. This road, steeped in atmosphere, was the scene of a dark episode in Dutch history: here, between 1572 and 1584, lived William I the Silent, a leader of the Dutch rebellion against Catholic Spain; here in 1584 the prince was assassinated by a Catholic fanatic, Balthasar Gerards.*

113 bottom right *Rising from the Markt are the pinnacles of the Marta Van Jessekerk.*

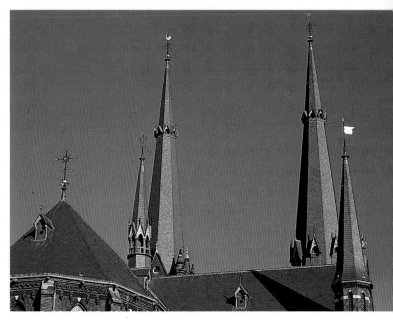

Rotterdam, a new life

114-115 *The railway station area was one of those most battered by the German air raids of 1940, but strangely the bombs spared the nearby Stadhuis (town hall), left almost intact. The facade of the town hall thus still serves as a backdrop to the Coolsingel, the avenue leading towards the town centre. The monument here in the foreground, by Marie Andressen, commemorates the victims of the war.*

115 top *The city hall of Rotterdam is the largest in the Netherlands. Although it was spared by the bombs, it is certainly not a symbol of the ancient city. It was only built at the beginning of this century, between 1914 and 1920. Inside is the famous large council room, embellished with numerous paintings by famous artists.*

115 centre *The Lijnbaan is the best-known and busiest street in the city: running in a straight line for over a mile and closed to automobile traffic, it is famous for having been the first true pedestrian area in the world, designed in 1953. But "Lijnbaan" is also the name of the huge shopping centre on the road, made to rational and modern standards and destined to become a model for various European cities. Other important shopping streets are the Van Oldebarneveldstraat and the already mentioned Coolsingel.*

115 bottom *Old houses dating from the last century that escaped the bombing and are now carefully restored, coexist in Rotterdam with the ultra modern skyscrapers in glass and concrete that rose from the ruins. The effect is sometimes unusual and even contradictory.*

116 top *After the war, the new Rotterdam was built in just twenty years thanks to the huge financial investment and the contribution of architects from all over the world. One of the most famous is Piet Blom (who created the renowned and eccentric "cubic houses"), Johannes Van Roode (designer of the first pedestrian zone in the world, the Lijnbaan) and Marcel Breuer (who designed the De Bijekorf stores). Thanks to their exceptional contribution, the city is modern and beautiful.*

116 centre *Most of the buildings built in Rotterdam during recent years according to the most scrupulous functional criteria have a very modern look. Anyway, despite the massive presence of steel, concrete and glass, the Dutch city is not characterized by the sad greyness typical of many modern cities.*

116 bottom *Euromast is a record-making tower: at 606 feet, it is the highest building not just in Rotterdam but in all The Netherlands. Indeed, on the flat Dutch landscape its summit is said to be the highest point in the country, although this is not true (in Limburg there are hills almost 1,000 feet high). Euromast was built in 1960 for telecommunications but then became a tourist attraction too: there is a restaurant on its panoramic terrace and even higher up is the Space adventure, a chamber with special effects where it is possible to experience the thrill of being launched into space on a rocket.*

116-117 *From the top of Euromast, looking northwards, Rotterdam appears as a sea of skyscrapers that hide the few period houses that escaped the war destruction. The city is constantly expanding, and not just upwards.*

118 *Despite the relentless economic and construction boom, Rotterdam is not only concrete: its city plan provides for green spaces according to criteria proportional to the cubic area of the surrounding buildings. The most important green space in the centre, simply called Park, is around Euromast, close to the River Meuse. Here, amidst lawns and trees, are five of the major city museums: the most important is the Boymans-Van Beuningen Museum, an eclectic picture gallery with masterpieces from all periods and all the countries of Europe. Among others are pictures by Monet, Van Gogh, Picasso, Munch and Kandinsky, as well as masterpieces of the Flemish school, of course. Just south of the park starts a tunnel leading to the other side of the Meuse.*

119 top *Born between the Rotte and the Meuse (Maas), the city of Erasmus had to come to terms with the rivers from the very first. Once the only problem was the floods, contained with the usual system of dykes. Then, as the town grew, the two waterways became an impediment even in normal times. Today much of the city has developed south of the Meuse. To assure a rapid passage between the two parts of Rotterdam, huge suspended bridges like that in the picture were built after the war. The main communication thoroughfare between the two sides is still however the Maastunnel passing below the river: over a mile long, a quarter of it below the level of the water, the tunnel has separate lanes for automobiles, bicycles and pedestrians. It is surprising that the tunnel, started in 1937, was completed in 1942, in the middle of the war.*

119 bottom *The port of Rotterdam, the largest in the world, lies partly on the Meuse and partly on an artificial branch of the river (Nieuwe Waterweg) made in 1872 and running straight to the sea. The piers are almost 25 miles long and cover a surface area of approximately 25 acres. The complex is divided into various goods sectors: those closest to the city are Waalhaven (minerals) and Maashaven (cereals); the farthest is the Europoort, inaugurated in 1958 on the sea, opposite the suburb of Hoek van Holland. This enormous maritime terminal is used by almost 500 shipping lines, with a passage of 300 million tons of goods per year. Most important of all, Rotterdam is the leading petroleum market and nearly all the crude oil coming into Europe from the Middle East arrives here before being sent to the oil refineries.*

Brabant and Limburg, frontier lands

120-121 *Dedicated to St. John and built between 1419 and 1525 (but the tower is prior to that), the cathedral of s'Hertogenbosch is a masterpiece of florid Gothic architecture. Above all it is the symbol of the tormented history of Brabant, the land standing on the boundary between different cultures. Born Catholic, in 1619 the church became Protestant, not returning to its original worship until 1810; its history reflects religious rivalry but also the troubled political events witnessed by the city.*

121 left *Impressive flying buttresses support the nave and transept, giving the structure a considerable vertical rise.*

121 right top *Internally the cathedral is richly decorated; nothing of the austere former church remains.*

121 bottom right *The cathedral of s'Hertogenbosch, whose choir is shown here in the picture, is the largest Gothic church in the Netherlands.*

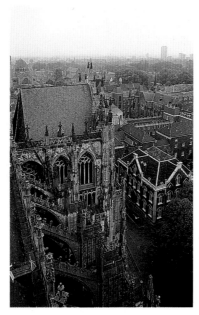

122-123 *Maastricht, the main city in Limburg, is famous for the treaty that abolished the internal European frontiers. But the city can also boast previous episodes in history: founded by the Romans 2,000 years ago, it was extremely prosperous in the Middle Ages and again in the 19th century, when it became the most important industrial town in the Netherlands, thanks to the coal mines nearby. Lying on the banks of the Meuse and around a Romanesque cathedral (St. Servaaskerk), it is now a peaceful commercial town. It is curious that the legendary D'Artagnan, the character in the famous novel "The Three Musketeers" by Alexandre Dumas, died beneath the town walls during the siege of the French army in 1673.*

Apeldoorn, the garden of kings

124 *Known as Het Loo, this is a huge palace-garden that monopolizes the landscape on the outskirts of Apeldoorn. The complex was built in 1685 for William III, Prince of Orange and King of England; after that, it was long the favourite residence of the Dutch royal family. Recently restored, Het Loo is now just a museum, conserving among other things a valuable collection of carriages.*

124-125 *The gardens and the external facades of Het Loo are full of statues and monumental fountains of a manifestly Italian influence. The overall structure, however, was inspired by French villas and palaces, Versailles in particular. The kings of The Netherlands lived for 300 years in these highly picturesque surroundings; the last was Queen Wilhelmina, who abdicated in 1948 and retired to Apeldoorn.*

126-127 *The castle of Heeswijk, erected in the 14th century but repeatedly altered, like many other Dutch fortresses, stands on an island surrounded by a moat.*

128 *The Netherlands is not famous for tulips alone; the vast greenhouses that dot the country also grow all kinds of roses and hundreds of other flower species.*